Vehicles On The Move

D1117757

Hovering Helicopters

Molly Aloian

🌳 **Crabtree Publishing Company**

www.crabtreebooks.com

Created by Bobbie Kalman

Author
Molly Aloian

Editorial director
Kathy Middleton

Project editor
Paul Challen

Editor
Adrianna Morganelli

Proofreaders
Rachel Stuckey
Crystal Sikkens

Photo research
Melissa McCLellan

Design
Tibor Choleva
Melissa McClellan

Production coordinators
Katherine Berti
Margaret Amy Salter

Prepress technicians
Katherine Berti
Margaret Amy Salter

Consultant
Erin Napier

Illustrations
All illustrations by Leif Peng

Photographs
Dreamstime.com: © Derek Gordon (title page); © Kitchner Bain (table of contents page); © Anthony Hathaway (page 5); © Keith Barlow (page 11); © Ice962 (pages 14–15); © Trondur (page 18); © Charles Mccarthy (page 19 top); © Arievdwolde (page 25); © Shibubu(page 26); © Tom Dowd (28 top); © Bambi L. Dingman (page 29 middle); © Brian Nguyen (30 top)
Shutterstock.com: © Artur Bogacki: front cover; © Rudchenko Liliia (blue sky); © Daniel Mazac (page 4); © Lukich (page 4 top); © Rob Byron (pages 6–7); © Christopher Sykes (page 8); © Ross Wallace (page 9); © Johan Knelsen (page 9 top); © Stephen Gibson (page 10); © Walter G Arce (page 11 top); © Jorg Hackemann (page 12); © Atlaspix (page 13); © Jan Martin Will (page 13 top); © Wessel du Plooy (page 16); © Tonylady (page 18 top); © David Hyde (page 19); © Monkey Business (page 20); © gary718 (page 21); © Ivan Cholakov Gostock-dot-net (page 21 top); © Roca (page 22 top); © Mircea Bezergheanu (pages 22-23); © Brian Finestone (23 top); © EuToch (pages 28–29); © Balazs Toth (page 29 top); © Lukich (page 30 bottom)
U.S. Defense Imagery: back cover, pages 17, 24
Public Domain: James Haseltine (US Air Force): page 31 top
NASA: page 31 bottom

Library and Archives Canada Cataloguing in Publication

Aloian, Molly
    Hovering helicopters / Molly Aloian.

(Vehicles on the move)
Includes index.
Issued also in an electronic format.
ISBN 978-0-7787-3048-4 (bound).--ISBN 978-0-7787-3062-0 (pbk.)

    1. Helicopters--Juvenile literature. I. Title. II. Series: Vehicles on the move

TL716.2.A46 2011   j629.133'352   C2010-904800-8

Library of Congress Cataloging-in-Publication Data

CIP available at Library of Congress

Crabtree Publishing Company
www.crabtreebooks.com   1-800-387-7650

Printed in the U.S.A./082010/BA20100709

Published in Canada
Crabtree Publishing
616 Welland Ave.
St. Catharines, ON
L2M 5V6

Published in the United States
Crabtree Publishing
PMB 59051
350 Fifth Avenue, 59th Floor
New York, New York 10118

Published in the United Kingdom
Crabtree Publishing
Maritime House
Basin Road North, Hove
BN41 1WR

Published in Australia
Crabtree Publishing
386 Mt. Alexander Rd.
Ascot Vale (Melbourne)
VIC 3032

Contents

High-flying helicopters

A helicopter is an aircraft. A helicopter does not have wings like other types of aircraft. Instead of wings, a helicopter has long blades called **rotors**. Unlike other types of aircraft, a helicopter can fly up, down, forward, backward, and sideways.

A helicopter's rotors spin rapidly above it, keeping it in the air and allowing it to fly in all directions.

Helpful helicopters

Helicopters can do many jobs. Some pilots fly helicopters into dangerous places to rescue people who are trapped or stranded. This type of helicopter is called a **search and rescue helicopter**. Other helicopters are used to carry loads of supplies to hard-to-reach places.

Sometimes, helicopters help in rescuing people who have had accidents while climbing mountains.

Take a closer look

Helicopters do jobs that no other aircraft can. Helicopters are made up of many parts. Each part of a helicopter does a different job.

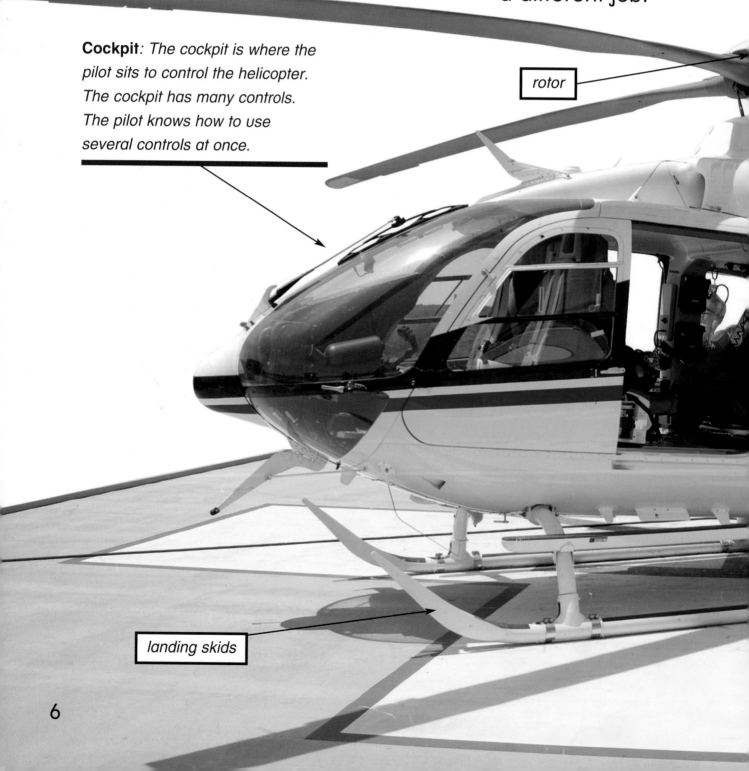

Cockpit: The cockpit is where the pilot sits to control the helicopter. The cockpit has many controls. The pilot knows how to use several controls at once.

rotor

landing skids

This helicopter is a medical helicopter. It can fly a sick person to a hospital and land safely and quickly on the hospital roof.

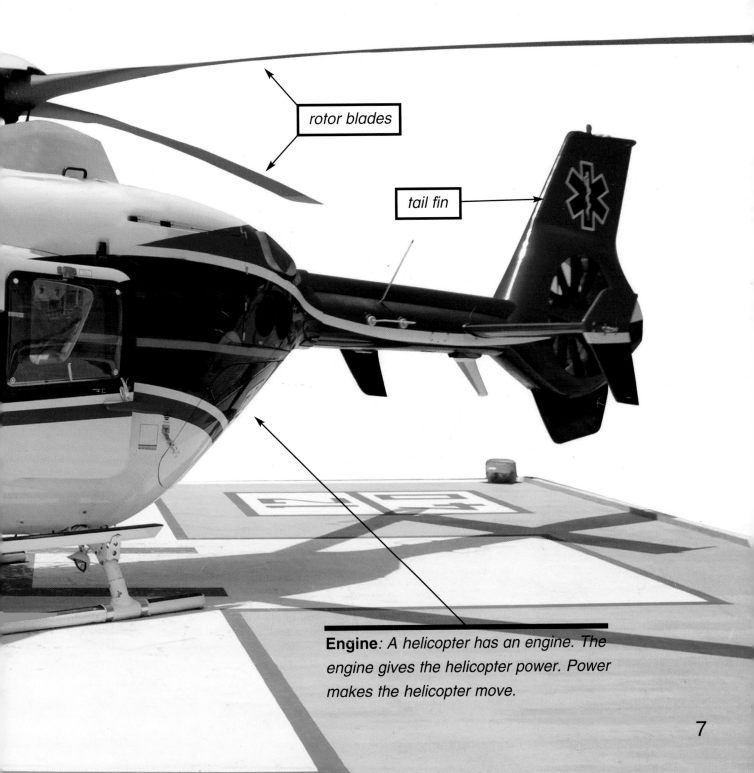

rotor blades

tail fin

Engine: *A helicopter has an engine. The engine gives the helicopter power. Power makes the helicopter move.*

Right on rotors

A helicopter has **rotors**. A large main rotor on top of the helicopter lifts the helicopter off of the ground. The engine powers the rotor and makes it spin. The helicopter can then lift into the air.

main rotor

The rotors sit at the very top of a helicopter. When they spin rapidly, they give the helicopter the lift it needs to leave the ground and fly.

Taking on torque

A smaller rotor on the back of the helicopter stops the helicopter from spinning out of control. If the main rotor is spinning in one direction, the helicopter will turn in the opposite direction. This is called **torque**. The small tail rotor stops the torque from the main rotor and allows the helicopter to fly straight.

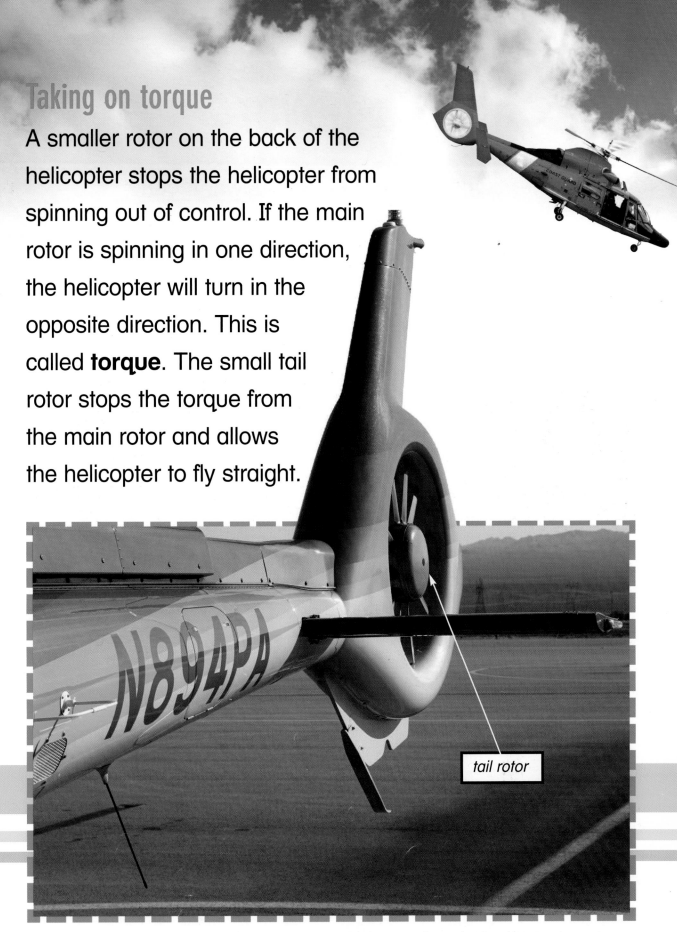

tail rotor

Unlike many vehicles, a helicopter gets it steering power from the back.

How to hover

A helicopter can fly straight up and down. It can also **hover**, or float in the air. As the rotor blades slice through the air, they create strong wind. This wind pushes downward, forcing the helicopter to move upward into the air. It can then fly higher or stay just above the ground.

It is easy to see the force that a helicopter produces—waves move out in all directions around the vehicle when it hovers over water.

Easy to land

A helicopter does not need a long runway to take off or land. It can hover for long periods of time and then land in many different places, including the top of an office building, the middle of a forest, or a highway.

Hospitals and businesses often use helicopters because they can land on rooftops in the middle of a crowded city.

Skids or wheels

Some helicopters land on **skids**. Others land on wheels. Smaller helicopters usually have skids. Skids weigh less than wheels do, so helicopters with skids can carry heavier loads than helicopters of the same size with wheels. Larger helicopters, such as military helicopters, often have wheels.

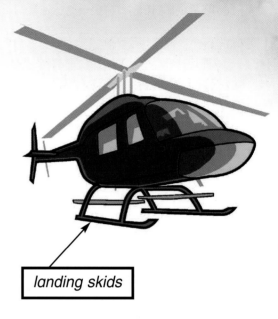

landing skids

Helicopters like this one are often used by fire departments and police forces to help with highway accidents.

Wheels out!

Some helicopters have wheels. Some wheels are **retractable**, which means they can pull back inside the helicopter when they are not being used.

A triangular block called a chock prevents a helicopter wheel from moving when not in use.

retractable wheels

This helicopter's wheels are out and ready for landing.

The need for speed

Helicopters cannot fly as fast as jets or airplanes, but they are usually faster than trucks, cars, or trains. The fastest helicopter in the world reached a record-breaking speed of nearly 250 miles per hour (402 km per hour). It was a modified Westland Lynx.

The Westland Lynx helicopter is one of the fastest helicopters in the world.

Get wind of this!

Many helicopters fly between 80 mph (129 KPH) and 170 mph (274 KPH).

Military helicopters have powerful engines. They can fly fast when they need to.

In combat

There are many types of helicopters. **Combat helicopters** have different jobs. They carry soldiers into battle or rescue injured soldiers and take them to hospitals. They can easily and quickly transport weapons and other goods from place to place.

Combat helicopters are harder for enemies to shoot down than jets and other aircraft.

Amazing Osprey

The V-22 Osprey is an amazing aircraft. It is what is considered a tiltrotor aircraft, both an airplane and a helicopter. The Osprey does not need a runway to take off or land, like an airplane, because it can land vertically, like a helicopter. The Osprey can also refuel in midair, as some airplanes do, so it can fly for longer periods of time. The Osprey is designed to land and take off on ships, as well as airplanes.

The V-22 Osprey can pick up pilots shot down in enemy territory and fly them back to safety. It is also used for combat and special operations.

At sea

Some helicopters can fly out to huge ships or **oil rigs** in the middle of oceans or seas. They land on platforms on the ships and rigs. The helicopter transports crew members, supplies, and important equipment needed for work at sea.

It is very difficult for a pilot to land a helicopter on a platform in the middle of a wavy ocean or sea. The pilot first has to hover above the water and try to follow the rhythm of the waves in order to land the helicopter safely.

Patrolling the coast

Special police and military forces patrol the coastlines of many countries. These coast guards use helicopters to rescue boats and ships that have run into trouble. They also use helicopters to watch over the coast from high in the air.

The U.S. Coast Guard uses helicopters to rescue people from sinking ships in stormy weather.

Air ambulances are helicopters that contain life-saving equipment, such as medicine, ventilators, and CPR equipment. They can pick up victims trapped in accidents on roads or highways and take them to the hospital.

A helicopter crew and medical workers move a patient from an air ambulance to a hospital.

The police use helicopters with spotlights to search for missing or wanted people in large, natural areas such as forests or marshes. It would take hours for a person to walk or drive through these large areas, but a helicopter can search people out in a matter of minutes.

From the ground, it would be impossible to spot a lost person in woods like these. But from high in the sky, searchers in a helicopter have a much better chance.

Into mountain regions

People use helicopters to fly into and out of mountain regions for heli-skiing. Heli-skiing is a popular mountain sport in North America, Asia, and Europe. Skiers or snowboarders are flown out to high mountains so they can ski or snowboard their way down.

Heli-skiers love the breathtaking scenery on mountains.

Safe skiing

These daredevils call the untouched snow on the mountains "powder." If the skiers or snowboarders get hurt or need help on their way down the powder, the helicopters are used to help them or fly them to safety.

A rescue worker flies under a helicopter with a patient in a rescue stretcher.

Carrying loads

Big, powerful helicopters have huge engines and can lift and carry heavy loads, such as cars or gigantic wooden logs, to and from places that are difficult for other vehicles to reach.

A CH-54 Skycrane helicopter picking up a piece of a dismantled airplane to remove it from the airfield

Get a load of this!

Heavy-lift helicopters that carry heavy loads, usually have two large main rotors that turn in opposite directions. They also have huge slings for carrying the loads and cargo hooks to attach the loads to the helicopters. The largest, most powerful helicopters can lift the weight of nearly six elephants!

If a military jeep cannot drive from one location to another, a helicopter can lift it to its destination.

Fighting fires

Some helicopters can be used to fight fires. During hot, dry summers, wildfires can start in forests and plains all over the world. The heat and smoke from these fires can be too intense for firefighters on the ground. Helicopters can fight fires from the air.

This helicopter is dropping water from a special bucket suspended on a cable.

Water drop

These helicopters can carry thousands of gallons of water to drop onto fires. The huge water tanks are located underneath the helicopter. These helicopters can also bring supplies, such as tools, pumps, and hoses, to safe places on the ground for firefighters to pick up.

This helicopter drops water from built-in water tanks.

In the news

Television and movie crews use helicopters to film overhead scenes in movies or television shows. Photographers can also take stunning pictures of animals, people, and places from helicopters in the air.

This pilot is flying a news helicopter. The helicopter transports news reporters from place to place so they can report news quickly.

Getting down

Flying low to the ground is dangerous in an airplane, but it is safe to do in a helicopter. Helicopters can fly low enough for people to film exciting cycling races from start to finish.

Reporters have a birds-eye view of a championship cycling race.

EXI
113

Into the future

Today, people are trying to combine the features of a helicopter with the speed of an airplane. For example, the V-22 Osprey can take off like a helicopter, but has the speed of an airplane. It is almost twice as fast as other helicopters!

The Bell-Boeing V-22 Osprey draws crowds wherever it goes because of its unique look and amazing flying abilities.

Shape-changer

Researchers at NASA (the National Aeronautics and Space Administration) are trying to make a helicopter with special shape-changing rotor blades that will be able to carry as many as 100 passengers and fly farther using the same amount of fuel.

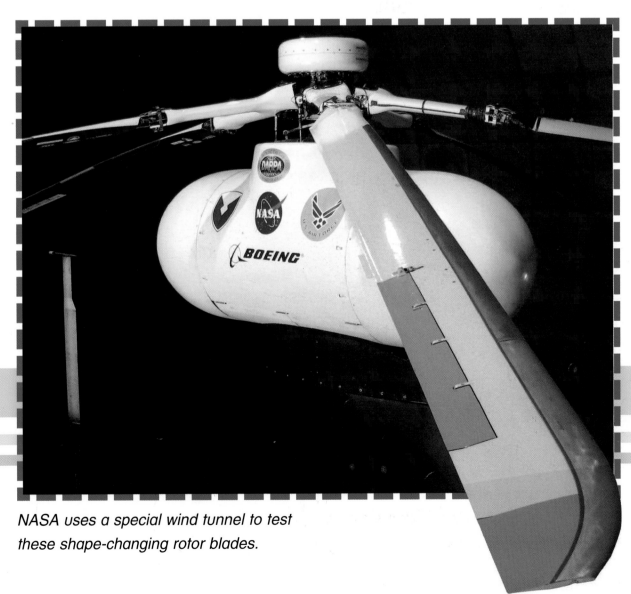

NASA uses a special wind tunnel to test these shape-changing rotor blades.

Words to know and Index

air ambulance
page 20

combat helicopters
pages 16–17

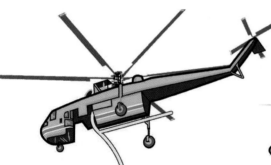

firefighting helicopters
pages 26–27

heavy-lift helicopters
page 25

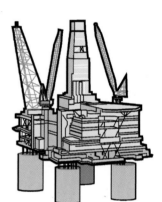

oil rig
page 18

police
page 21

**search and rescue
helicopter**
page 5

skids
pages 6, 12